The Best
BROWNIES
& BARS

The Best
BROWNIES
& BARS

Chewies, Crumbles, Crunchies, and Other Cakey Cookies

By Gregg R. Gillespie

Black Dog
& Leventhal
Publishers
New York

Copyright © 2002 by Black Dog & Leventhal Publishers, Inc.
Recipes copyright © 2002 by Gregg R. Gillespie

All rights reserved. No part of this book may be reproduced in any form or by any electronic or mechanical means including information storage and retrieval systems without the written permission of the copyright holder.

Published by
Black Dog & Leventhal Publishers, Inc.
151 West 19th Street
New York, NY 10011

Distributed by
Workman Publishing
708 Broadway
New York, NY 10003

Manufactured in Spain

ISBN 1-57912-291-4

Library of Congress Cataloging-in-Publication Data is on file and available from Black Dog & Leventhal Publishers, Inc.

Cover and interior design by 27.12 Design, Ltd.
Interior layout by Sheila Hart Design, Inc.
Photography by Peter Barry

g f e d c b a

CONTENTS

Ambrosia Bars............................7
Apple Bars 8
Apple Butter-Oatmeal Bars..........9
Apple Spice Bars 10
Applesauce Date Bars 11
Apricot Bars 12
Baked Cheesecake Bars 13
Banana Chip Bars 14
Banana Coconut Bars 15
Basic Fudge Brownies................16
Bittersweet Brownies 17
Blackberry Meringue Bars 18
Blond Brownies.........................19
Blueberry Bars...........................20
Brandy Alexander Brownies.......21
Brown-and-White Brownies 22
Brownies I.................................23
Brownies II 24
Butterscotch Bars......................25
Butterscotch Brownies 26
Butterscotch Cheesecake Bars...27
Butterscotch Chews..................28
Butterscotch Squares 29
Caramel Bars 30

Cashew Bars.............................31
Cashew Caramel Cookies 32
Cashew Granola Bars................33
Cheesecake Cookies 34
Cherry-Almond Squares............35
Cherry Squares 36
Chewy Pecan Bars 37
Chocolate Chip Bar Cookies 38
Chocolate Chip Squares............39
Chocolate Delight Bars 40
Chunky Chocolate Brownies 41
Citrus Bars 42
Coconut Brownies 43
Coconut Caramel Bars 44
Coconut Chewies 45
Date Honey Fingers...................46
Dutch Crunch
    Applesauce Bars 47
English Toffee Bars....................48
Fruit-Filled Oatcakes..................49
Fruit Meringue Bars 50
Fudge Brownies I 51
Fudge Brownies II......................52
Fudge Brownies III.....................53

Ginger Bars 54	Mocha Coffee Brownies 75
Graham Cracker Brownies I 55	No-Bake Oatmeal Bars 76
Graham Cracker Brownies II 56	Orange Bars 77
Granola Bars 57	Orange Cranberry Bars 78
Gumdrop Bars 58	Peanut Butter-Banana Squares .. 79
Hazelnut Squares 59	Peanut Butter Bars I 80
Hello Dolly Cookies 60	Peanut Butter Bars II 81
Hiker's Treats 61	Pumpkin Bars 82
Honey Brownies 62	Raisin Bars 83
Honey Date Bars 63	Rocky Road Bars 84
Jam Squares 64	Seven-Layer Cookies 85
Kentucky Pecan Bars 65	Some-More Bars 86
Krispies 66	Spice Bars 87
Lemon Bars I 67	Strawberry Meringue Bars 88
Lemon Bars II 68	Teatime Favorites 89
Lemon Bars III 69	Torta Fregolotti 90
Macadamia Nut Bars 70	Tropical Bars 91
Magic Bars 71	Tropical Fruit Bars 92
Marbled Cream Cheese Brownies 72	Walnut Bars 93
Meringue-Topped Brownies 73	Walnut Squares 94
Mint Brownies 74	Zucchini Bars 95

AMBROSIA BARS

Yield: 2 to 3 dozen

2 cups all-purpose flour
½ tsp. baking powder
½ tsp. baking soda
¼ tsp. salt
¾ cup vegetable shortening
1 cup packed light brown sugar
1 large egg
¼ cup fresh orange juice
1 tbsp. grated orange zest
1 cup (6 oz.) butterscotch chips
1 cup shredded coconut

1. Preheat the oven to 350 degrees. Grease a 13 by 9-inch baking pan.
2. Combine the flour, baking powder, baking soda, and salt.
3. In a large bowl, cream the vegetable shortening and brown sugar. Beat in the egg, orange juice, and zest. Gradually blend in the dry ingredients. Fold in the butterscotch chips and coconut.
4. Spread the batter evenly in the prepared pan.
5. Bake for 25 to 30 minutes, or until the top is a golden brown. Cool in the pan on a rack before cutting into large or small squares.

APPLE BARS

Yield: 1 to 2 dozen

¾ cup all-purpose flour
½ tsp. baking powder
¼ tsp. baking soda
½ tsp. ground ginger
¼ tsp. ground nutmeg
⅓ cup vegetable shortening
¾ cup granulated sugar
2 large eggs
1 cup diced, peeled apples
topping
1½ tsp. granulated sugar
½ cup ground cinnamon

1. Preheat the oven to 350 degrees.
2. Combine the flour, baking powder, baking soda, ginger, and nutmeg.
3. In a large bowl, cream the vegetable shortening and sugar. Beat in the eggs. Gradually blend in the dry ingredients. Fold in the apples.
4. Spread the dough evenly in an ungreased 9-inch square baking pan.
5. Combine the cinnamon and sugar for the topping. Sprinkle evenly over the dough.
6. Bake for 25 to 30 minutes, or until firm to the touch. Let cool in the pan on a rack before cutting into large or small bars.

Baking note: Add ½ cup raisins and/or ½ cup chopped nuts to the dough if desired.

APPLE BUTTER-OATMEAL BARS

Yield: 2 to 3 dozen

⅔ cup all-purpose flour
½ tsp. baking powder
¼ tsp. salt
½ cup vegetable shortening
½ cup apple butter
½ cup packed dark brown sugar
1 large egg
½ tsp. baking soda
1 tbsp. warm water
1 cup rolled oats
1 cup flaked coconut (optional)

1. Preheat the oven to 350 degrees. Grease a 13 by 9-inch baking pan.
2. Combine the flour, baking powder and salt.
3. In a large bowl, cream the vegetable shortening, apple butter, and brown sugar. Beat in the egg.
4. Dissolve the baking soda in the warm water and add to the creamed mixture, beating until smooth. Gradually blend in the dry ingredients. Fold in the oats and coconut.
5. Spread the mixture evenly in the prepared pan.
6. Bake for 15 to 20 minutes, or until lightly colored. Cool in the pan on a rack before cutting into large or small bars.

Baking note: If you like chocolate, add chocolate chips to the dough and drizzle melted chocolate over the top of the cooked cookies.

APPLE-SPICE BARS

Yield: 1 to 2 dozen

1½ cups all-purpose flour
½ tsp. baking powder
½ tsp. ground nutmeg
½ tsp. ground ginger
¼ tsp. salt
⅔ cup vegetable shortening
1½ cups granulated sugar
4 large eggs
½ tsp. baking soda
1 tbsp. warm water
1 cup diced, peeled apples
topping
¼ cup granulated sugar
1 tsp. ground cinnamon

1. Preheat the oven to 350 degrees. Grease a 13 by 9-inch baking pan.
2. Combine the flour, baking powder, spices, and salt.
3. In a large bowl, cream the vegetable shortening and sugar. Beat in the eggs.
4. Dissolve the baking soda in the warm water and add to the egg mixture, beating until smooth. Gradually blend in the dry ingredients. Fold in the apples.
5. Spread the mixture evenly in the prepared pan. Combine the sugar and cinnamon for the topping and sprinkle evenly over the cookies.
6. Bake for 25 to 30 minutes, or until top is lightly browned. Cool in the pan on a rack before cutting into large or small bars.

APPLESAUCE DATE BARS

Yield: 2 to 3 dozen

2 cups all-purpose flour
1 tsp. ground cinnamon
½ tsp. ground cardamom
Pinch of salt
¾ cup vegetable shortening
1 cup granulated sugar
2 tsp. baking soda

1 tbsp. warm water
2 large eggs
2 cups unsweetened applesauce
1 cup pitted dates, chopped
1 cup walnuts, chopped

1. Preheat the oven to 350 degrees. Grease a 13 by 9-inch baking pan.
2. Combine the flour, cinnamon, cardamom, and salt.
3. In a large bowl, cream the vegetable shortening and sugar.
4. Dissolve the baking soda in the warm water and add to the creamed mixture, beating until smooth. Beat in the eggs. Beat in the applesauce. Gradually blend in the dry ingredients. Fold in the dates and walnuts.
5. Spread the mixture evenly in the prepared pan.
6. Bake for 25 to 30 minutes, or until golden brown on top. Cool in the pan on a rack before cutting into large or small bars.

Baking note: For a decorative touch, frost these with vanilla icing, and drizzle dark chocolate icing over the top.

APRICOT BARS

Yield: 2 to 3 dozen

1¾ cups all-purpose flour
½ cup almonds, ground fine
½ tsp. salt
¾ cup vegetable shortening
¾ cup powdered sugar
½ tsp. almond extract

filling
One jar (12 oz.) apricot preserves
½ cup glacé cherries, diced
1½ tsp. brandy

1. Preheat the oven to 350 degrees.
2. Combine the flour, almonds, and salt.
3. In a large bowl, cream the vegetable shortening and powdered sugar. Beat in the almond extract. Gradually blend in the dry ingredients.
4. Set aside 1 cup of the almond mixture for the topping. Spread the remaining mixture evenly over the bottom of an ungreased 13 by 9-inch baking pan.
5. To make the filling, combine the apricot preserves, cherries, and brandy in a small bowl, and stir until well blended. Spread the filling evenly over the almond mixture. Crumble the reserved almond mixture over the filling.
6. Bake for 30 to 35 minutes, until the edges are dark golden brown. Cut into large or small bars while still warm, and cool in the pan on a rack.

BAKED CHEESECAKE BARS

Yield: 1 to 2 dozen

crust

1 cup all-purpose flour
⅓ cup packed light brown sugar
⅓ cup vegetable shortening

filling

2 large eggs
1 pound cream cheese, at room temperature
½ cup granulated sugar
2 tbsp. fresh lemon juice
1 tbsp. marsala

1. Preheat the oven to 350 degrees.
2. To make the crust, combine the flour and brown sugar in a bowl. Cut in the vegetable shortening until the mixture resembles coarse crumbs.
3. Press the mixture evenly into the bottom of a 9-inch square baking pan. Bake for 15 minutes.
4. Meanwhile, make the filling: in a large bowl, beat the eggs until thick and light-colored. Beat in the cream cheese and sugar until smooth. Beat in the lemon juice and marsala.
5. Spread the filling evenly over the warm crust. Bake for 20 minutes longer, or until firm to the touch.
6. Cool in the pan on a rack before cutting into large or small bars.

Baking note: A teaspoon of almond extract can be used in place of the marsala.

BANANA CHIP BARS

Yield: 1 to 2 dozen

2 cups all-purpose flour
2 tsp. baking powder
½ tsp. salt
¾ cup vegetable shortening
1 cup granulated sugar
¼ cup packed light brown sugar

1 large egg
1 tsp. vanilla extract
1 cup mashed bananas
1 cup (6 oz.) semi-sweet chocolate chips

1. Preheat the oven to 350 degrees. Grease a 13 by 9-inch baking pan.
2. Combine the flour, baking powder, and salt.
3. In a large bowl, cream the vegetable shortening and both sugars. Beat in the egg and vanilla extract. Beat in the bananas. Gradually blend in the dry ingredients. Fold in the chocolate chips.
4. Spread the mixture evenly in the prepared pan.
5. Bake for 25 to 30 minutes, until golden brown on top. Cool in the pan on a rack before cutting into large or small bars.

Baking note: A packaged banana cream frosting goes very well with these bars.

BANANA COCONUT BARS

Yield: 2 to 3 dozen

1¾ cups all-purpose flour
2 tsp. baking powder
1 tsp. baking soda
⅓ cup vegetable shortening
2 to 3 medium bananas, mashed

1 large egg
½ cup milk
¼ tsp. fresh lemon juice
1½ cups flaked coconut

1. Preheat the oven to 350 degrees. Grease a 13 by 9-inch baking pan.
2. Combine the flour, baking powder, and baking soda.
3. In a large bowl, beat the vegetable shortening and bananas until smooth. Beat in the egg, milk, and lemon juice. Gradually blend in the dry ingredients. Fold in 1 cup of the coconut.
4. Spread the mixture evenly in the prepared pan. Sprinkle the remaining ½ cup coconut over the top.
5. Bake for 15 to 20 minutes, until the top is lightly colored, and a toothpick inserted into the center comes out clean. Cool in the pan on a rack before cutting into large or small bars.

BASIC FUDGE BROWNIES

Yield: 1 to 2 dozen

½ cup plus 2 tbsp. vegetable shortening
2 tbsp. unsweetened cocoa powder
1 cup granulated sugar
2 large eggs
1 tsp. vanilla extract
½ cup all-purpose flour

1. Preheat the oven to 350 degrees. Grease a 9-inch square baking pan.
2. Combine the vegetable shortening and cocoa in the top of a double boiler and heat over low heat, stirring occasionally, until the shortening is melted.
3. Remove from the heat and stir in the sugar. Stir in the eggs and vanilla extract until well blended. Stir in the flour.
4. Spread the mixture evenly in the prepared pan.
5. Bake for 18 to 20 minutes, until a toothpick inserted in the center comes out clean. Cool in the pan on a rack before cutting into large or small bars.

Baking note: When cool, these can be spread with chocolate glaze and sprinkled with chopped walnuts before being cut into bars.

BITTERSWEET BROWNIES

Yield: 1 to 3 dozen

2 oz. unsweetened chocolate, chopped
½ cup all-purpose flour
1 tsp. baking soda
¼ tsp. salt
½ cup vegetable shortening
¾ cup granulated sugar
2 large eggs
1 tsp. vanilla extract
1½ cups pecans, chopped

1. Preheat the oven to 350 degrees. Grease a 9-inch square baking pan.
2. Melt the chocolate in a double boiler over low heat, stirring until smooth. Remove from the heat.
3. Combine the flour, baking powder, and salt.
4. In a large bowl, cream the vegetable shortening and sugar. Beat in the eggs and vanilla extract. Beat in the melted chocolate. Gradually blend in the dry ingredients. Stir in the pecans.
5. Spread the mixture evenly in the prepared pan.
6. Bake for 20 to 25 minutes, until a toothpick inserted in the center comes out clean. Cool in the pan on a rack.
7. Frost with chocolate frosting and cut into large or small bars.

BLACKBERRY MERINGUE BARS

Yield: 3 to 4 dozen

crust
¾ cup vegetable shortening
¾ cup granulated sugar
2 large eggs yolks
1½ cups all-purpose flour
topping
2 large egg whites
½ cup granulated sugar
1 cup almond, chopped
1 cup blackberry purée, unstrained
1 cup shaved fresh coconut (see Baking note)

1. Preheat the oven to 350 degrees.
2. To make the crust, in a large bowl, cream the vegetable shortening and sugar. Beat in the egg yolks. Gradually blend in the flour.
3. Spread the mixture evenly in the bottom of an ungreased 13 by 9-inch baking pan. Bake for 15 minutes.
4. Meanwhile, make the topping: In a medium bowl, beat the egg whites into stiff peaks. Beat in the sugar. Fold in the nuts.
5. Spread the blackberry purée over the warm crust. Sprinkle with the coconut. Spread the meringue evenly over the top.
6. Bake for 20 to 25 minutes longer, until the topping is set. Cool in the pan on a rack before cutting into large or small bars.

Baking note: The blackberry purée can be fresh, canned, frozen, preserved, or a compote. If you do not have fresh coconut available packaged flaked coconut can be used. These cookies can be made with almost any type of berry. If desired, add ¼ teaspoon almond extract to the crust for subtle flavor.

BLOND BROWNIES

Yield: 1 to 3 dozen

2⅔ cups all-purpose flour
2½ tsp. baking powder
½ tsp. salt
⅔ cup vegetable shortening
2 cups packed light brown sugar

3 large eggs
1 tsp. vanilla extract
1 cup (6 oz.) semi-sweet chocolate chips

1. Preheat the oven to 375 degrees. Grease a 9-inch square baking pan.
2. Combine the flour, baking powder, and salt.
3. Melt the vegetable shortening in a medium saucepan. Stir in the brown sugar and cook over low heat for 10 minutes. Remove from the heat.
4. Add the eggs one at a time, beating well after each addition. Beat in the vanilla extract. Gradually blend in the dry ingredients. Stir in the chocolate chips.
5. Spread the batter evenly in the prepared pan.
6. Bake for 12 to 15 minutes, until a toothpick inserted in the center comes out clean. Cool in the pan on a rack before cutting into large or small bars.

Baking note: A creamy chocolate frosting flavored with 1 or 2 drops of mint extract goes very well with these bars. Using an 8-inch square baking pan will produce a thicker, cake-type brownie; a 13 by 9-inch baking pan will produce a thinner, chewier brownie.

BLUEBERRY BARS

Yield: 3 to 4 dozen

crust
½ cup granulated sugar
16 graham crackers, crushed
¼ cup vegetable shortening
filling
2 large eggs
8 oz. cream cheese, at room temperature
½ cup granulated sugar
½ tsp. almond extract
topping
12 oz. blueberries
2 tbsp. cornstarch
½ cup water
1 tsp. fresh lemon juice

1. Preheat the oven to 350 degrees. Lightly grease a 13 by 9-inch baking pan.
2. To make the crust, combine the sugar and vegetable shortening in a medium bowl. Add the graham crackers and work the mixture with your fingertips until crumbly. Press the mixture evenly into the prepared baking pan.
3. To make the filling, combine the eggs, cream cheese, sugar, and almond extract in a bowl and beat until smooth. Spread evenly over the crust.
4. Bake for 15 to 18 minutes, until firm to the touch. Cool in the pan on a wire rack.
5. Meanwhile, make the topping: Heat the blueberries on top of a double boiler over medium heat. Add the cornstarch, water, and lemon juice. Continue cooking over medium heat until the mixture is about as thick as mayonnaise. Remove from the heat and let cool.
6. Spread the blueberry mixture over the top of the cooled cookies. Refrigerate for 15 to 20 minutes before cutting into large or small bars.

Baking note: Vanilla wafers may be substituted for the graham crackers.

BRANDY ALEXANDER BROWNIES

Yield: 2 to 3 dozen

⅔ cup all-purpose flour
1 tbsp. unsweetened cocoa powder
½ tsp. baking powder
¼ tsp. salt

½ cup vegetable shortening
¾ cup granulated sugar
2 large eggs
2 tbsp. crème de cacao
2 tbsp. brandy

1. Preheat the oven to 350 degrees. Grease a 9-inch square baking pan.
2. Combine the flour, cocoa powder, baking powder, and salt.
3. In a large bowl, cream the vegetable shortening and sugar. Beat in the eggs. Beat in the crème de cacao and brandy. Gradually blend in the dry ingredients.
4. Spread the dough evenly in the prepared baking pan.
5. Bake for 20 to 25 minutes, until the top is lightly colored. Cool in the pan on a wire rack before cutting into large or small bars.

BROWN-AND-WHITE BROWNIES

Yield: 2 to 3 dozen

1 tbsp. vegetable shortening
¼ cup granulated sugar
1 large egg
¾ cup milk
½ tsp. vanilla extract
2 cups packaged cookie mix
⅓ cup chocolate syrup
1 cup (6 oz.) white chocolate chips
½ cup (3 oz.) semi-sweet chocolate chips

1. Preheat the oven to 375 degrees. Lightly grease a 9-inch square baking pan.
2. In a large bowl, cream the vegetable shortening and sugar. Beat in the eggs. Beat in the milk and vanilla extract. Gradually blend in the cookie mix. Transfer half the batter to another bowl.
3. For the brown layer, beat the chocolate syrup into half the batter. Stir in the white chocolate chips. Spread the mixture evenly in the prepared baking pan.
4. For the white layer, stir the semi-sweet chocolate chips into the remaining batter. Spread evenly over the dark layer.
5. Bake for 12 to 15 minutes, or until a toothpick inserted in the center comes out clean. Cool in the pan on a wire rack before cutting into large or small bars.

BROWNIES I
Yield: 1 to 2 dozen

4 oz. unsweetened chocolate, chopped
¾ cup vegetable shortening
2 cups granulated sugar
1 tsp. vanilla extract
3 large eggs
1 cup all-purpose flour
1 cup walnuts, chopped fine

1. Preheat the oven to 350 degrees. Lightly grease a 13 by 9-inch baking pan.
2. In a large saucepan, melt the unsweetened chocolate and vegetable shortening over low heat, stirring until smooth. Remove from the heat and beat in the sugar and vanilla extract. Beat in the eggs. Gradually blend in the flour. Fold in the walnuts. Spread the batter evenly in the prepared baking pan.
3. Bake for 35 to 40 minutes, until a toothpick inserted in the center comes out clean. Cool in the pan on a wire rack before cutting into large or small bars.

BROWNIES II

Yield: 1 to 2 dozen

½ cup all-purpose flour
½ tsp. salt
¼ cup vegetable shortening
2 oz. semi-sweet chocolate, chopped
1 cup granulated sugar
1 tsp. vanilla extract
2 large eggs
1 cup raisins (optional)
1 cup miniature marshmallows (optional)

1. Preheat the oven to 325 degrees. Lightly grease an 8-inch square baking pan.
2. Combine the flour and salt.
3. In a double boiler, melt the vegetable shortening and chocolate over low heat, stirring until smooth. Remove from the heat and beat in the sugar and vanilla extract. Beat in the eggs. Gradually blend in the dry ingredients. Fold in the optional raisins and marshmallows. Spread the batter evenly in the prepared baking pan.
4. Bake for 20 to 25 minute, until a toothpick inserted in the center comes out clean. Cut into large or small squares while still warm and cool in the pan on a wire rack.

BUTTERSCOTCH BARS

Yield: 2 to 3 dozen

2 cups all-purpose flour
2 tsp. baking powder
½ cup vegetable shortening
2 cups packed light brown sugar
2 large eggs
1 tsp. vanilla extract
1 cup shredded coconut
1 cup walnuts, chopped

1. Preheat the oven to 350 degrees. Lightly grease a 13 by 9-inch baking pan.
2. Combine the flour and baking powder.
3. In a large bowl, cream the vegetable shortening and brown sugar. Beat in the eggs. Beat in the vanilla extract. Gradually blend in the dry ingredients. Fold in the coconut and walnuts. Spread the mixture evenly in the prepared pan.
4. Bake for 25 to 30 minutes, until a toothpick inserted in the center comes out clean. Cut into large or small bars and cool in the pan on a wire rack.

BUTTERSCOTCH BROWNIES

Yield: 2 to 3 dozen

1½ cups all-purpose flour
2 tsp. baking powder
¼ tsp. salt
⅔ cup vegetable shortening
2 cups packed light brown sugar

2 large eggs
1 tsp. almond extract
1 cup almonds, chopped
¼ cup sliced almonds

1. Preheat the oven to 350 degrees. Lightly grease a 9-inch square baking pan.
2. Combine the flour, baking powder, and salt.
3. In a large bowl, cream the vegetable shortening and brown sugar. Beat in the eggs. Beat in the almond extract. Gradually blend in the dry ingredients. Stir in the chopped almonds.
4. Spread the batter evenly in the prepared baking pan. Sprinkle the sliced almonds over the top and press down lightly.
5. Bake for 30 to 35 minutes, until firm and a toothpick inserted in the center comes out clean. Cool in the pan on a wire rack before cutting into large or small bars.

BUTTERSCOTCH CHEESECAKE BARS

Yield: 1 to 2 dozen

crust
- ¾ cup butterscotch chips
- ⅓ cup butter, at room temperature
- 2 cups graham cracker crumbs
- 1 cup walnut, ground fine

filling
- 8 oz. cream cheese, at room temperature
- 1 can (14 oz.) sweetened condensed milk
- 1 large egg
- 1 tsp. vanilla extract

1. Preheat the oven to 350 degrees. Lightly grease a 13 by 9-inch baking pan.
2. To make the crust, melt the butterscotch chips and butter in a medium saucepan, stirring until smooth. Remove from the heat and blend in the graham cracker crumbs and walnuts. Spread half the mixture evenly into the bottom of the prepared baking pan.
3. To make the filling, beat the cream cheese and condensed milk together in a small bowl. Beat in the egg and vanilla extract. Pour this mixture over the crust.
4. Spread the remaining crust mixture over the filling.
5. Bake for 25 to 30 minutes, until a knife inserted into the center comes out clean. Cool in the pan on a wire rack before cutting into large or small bars.

BUTTERSCOTCH CHEWS

Yield: 1 to 2 dozen

2 cups all-purpose flour
2 tsp. baking powder
¼ tsp. salt
½ cup vegetable shortening

2 cups packed light brown sugar
2 large eggs
½ tsp. vanilla extract
1⅓ cups sliced almonds

1. Preheat the oven to 350 degrees. Lightly grease a 9-inch square baking pan.
2. Combine the flour, baking powder, and salt.
3. In a large bowl, cream the vegetable shortening and sugar. Beat in the eggs. Beat in the vanilla extract. Gradually blend in the dry ingredients.
4. Spread the mixture evenly in the prepared baking pan. Sprinkle the almonds over the top and press down gently.
5. Bake for 20 to 25 minutes, until firm to the touch. Cool in the pan on a wire rack before cutting into large or small bars.

BUTTERSCOTCH SQUARES

Yield: 1 to 2 dozen

1¼ cup all-purpose flour
1 tsp. baking powder
¼ tsp. salt
½ cup vegetable shortening

½ cup peanut butter
1½ packed light brown sugar
2 large eggs
1 tsp. vanilla extract

1. Preheat the oven to 350 degrees. Lightly grease a 9-inch square baking pan.
2. Combine the flour, baking powder, and salt.
3. In a medium saucepan, combine the vegetable shortening, peanut butter, brown sugar and heat over medium heat, stirring, until the shortening melts and the sugar dissolves. Remove from the heat and let cool slightly.
4. Beat the eggs into the peanut butter mixture. Beat in the vanilla extract. Gradually blend in the dry ingredients.
5. Spread the mixture evenly in the prepared baking pan.
6. Bake for 25 to 30 minutes, or until a toothpick inserted in the center comes out clean. Cool in the pan on a wire rack before cutting into large or small bars.

CARAMEL BARS

Yield: 1 to 2 dozen

1 package (14 oz.) caramels (light or dark)
⅔ cup evaporated milk
¾ cup vegetable shortening
1 package German chocolate cake mix
1 cup peanuts, chopped
1 cup (6 oz.) semi-sweet chocolate chips

1. Preheat the oven to 350 degrees. Lightly grease a 9-inch square baking pan.
2. In the top of a double boiler, melt the caramel candy with ⅓ cup of the evaporated milk, stirring until smooth. Remove from the heat.
3. In a large bowl, combine the vegetable shortening and cake mix and beat until smooth. Beat in the milk and stir in the peanuts. The mixture will be crumbly.
4. Press half of the cake mixture into the prepared baking pan. Bake for 8 minutes.
5. Sprinkle the chocolate chips over the warm dough. Spread the caramel mixture over the chocolate chips and spread the remaining cake mixture over the caramel layer.
6. Bake for 18 to 20 minutes longer, until firm to the touch. Cool in the pan on a wire rack before cutting into large or small bars.

CASHEW BARS

Yield: 2 to 3 dozen

2 cups all-purpose flour
1 cup cashews, ground fine
2 tsp.s baking powder
1 tsp. baking soda
1 tsp. ground nutmeg

½ cup vegetable shortening
3 large eggs
½ cup mashed bananas
½ cup cashews, chopped

1. Preheat the oven to 350 degrees. Lightly grease a 13 by 9-inch baking pan.
2. Combine the flour, ground cashews, baking powder, baking soda, and nutmeg.
3. In a large bowl, beat the vegetable shortening and eggs together. Beat in the bananas. Gradually blend in the dry ingredients
4. Spread the mixture evenly in the prepared baking pan. Sprinkle the chopped cashews over the batter and press down gently.
5. Bake for 18 to 20 minutes, or until a toothpick inserted in the center comes out clean. Cool in the pan on a wire rack before cutting into large or small bars.

CASHEW CARAMEL COOKIES

Yield: 1 to 2 dozen

¾ cup all-purpose flour
½ tsp. baking powder
¼ tsp. salt
2 large eggs
½ cup granulated sugar
2 tbsp. light brown sugar
½ cup cashews, chopped

topping
2 tbsp. butter
1 tbsp. evaporated milk
2 tbsp. light brown sugar
½ cup cashews, chopped

1. Preheat the oven to 350 degrees. Lightly grease a 9-inch square baking pan.
2. Combine the flour, baking powder, and salt.
3. In a large bowl, beat the eggs, and both sugars together until thick. Add the cashews. Gradually blend in the dry ingredients.
4. Spread the dough evenly in the prepared baking pan. Bake 25 minutes.
5. Meanwhile, make the topping in a saucepan: Combine all the ingredients and cook, stirring until smooth. Remove from the heat.
6. Preheat the broiler.
7. Spread the topping over the warm cookies and place under the broiler for 1 minute, or until the topping starts to bubble. Cut into large or small bars while still warm, and cool in the pan on a rack.

CASHEW GRANOLA BARS

Yield: 3 to 4 dozen

6 cups rolled oats
1 cup shredded coconuts
1 cup wheat germ
1 cup golden raisins
½ cup sunflower seeds, shelled
¼ cup sesame seeds, toasted

1 tsp. ground allspice
1 cup honey
¾ cup canola oil
⅓ cup water
1½ tsp. vanilla extract

1. Preheat the oven to 350 degrees. Lightly grease a 13 by 9-inch baking pan.
2. In a large bowl, combine the oats, coconuts, wheat germ, raisins, sunflower seeds, sesame seeds, and allspice.
3. In a medium saucepan, combine the honey, oil, water, and vanilla extract and heat until warm.
4. Pour over the dry ingredients and blend thoroughly. Spread the mixture evenly in the prepared baking pan.
5. Bake for 30 to 40 minutes, until firm and no longer sticking. Cut into large and small bars while still warm, and cool in the pan on a wire rack.

CHEESECAKE COOKIES

Yield: 1 to 3 dozen

crust
½ cup canola oil
¼ cup powdered sugar
24 gingersnaps, crushed

filling
1 pound cream cheese, at room temperature
½ cup granulated sugar
2 large eggs
1 tbsp. fresh lemon juice
1 tbsp. marsala
1 tbsp. honey
¼ tsp. ground allspice

1. Preheat the oven to 375 degrees.
2. To make the crust, beat the canola oil and powdered sugar together in a large bowl. Gradually work in the crushed gingersnaps.
3. Press the mixture evenly into an ungreased 9-inch square baking pan.
4. Bake for about 6 minutes.
5. Meanwhile, make the filling: In a large bowl, beat the cream cheese and sugar until creamy. Beat in the eggs. Beat in the lemon juice, marsala, honey, and allspice.
6. Spread the filling over the hot crust. Bake for 12 to 15 minutes longer, until set. Cool in the pan on a wire rack before cutting into large or small bars.

Baking note: For dessert, serve cut into large bars with sliced strawberries and whipped cream.

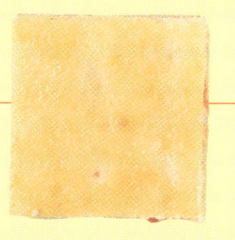

CHERRY ALMOND SQUARES

Yield: 1 to 2 dozen

crust
1 cup all-purpose flour
¼ tsp. salt
½ cup vegetable shortening
⅓ cup powdered sugar

topping
3 oz. cream cheese
½ cup crumbled almond paste
1 large egg
½ cup red maraschino cherries, chopped

1. Preheat the oven to 350 degrees.
2. Combine the flour and salt.
3. To make the crust, cream the vegetable shortening and powdered sugar in a large bowl. Gradually blend in the dry ingredients. The mixture will be crumbly.
4. Press the mixture evenly into the bottom of an ungreased 9-inch square baking pan. Bake for 15 minutes.
5. Meanwhile, make the topping: In a large bowl, beat the cream cheese and almond paste until smooth and creamy. Beat in the egg. Fold in the maraschino cherries.
6. Spread the topping over the warm crust. Bake for 15 minutes longer, until set. Cool in the pan on a wire rack before cutting into large or small bars.

CHERRY SQUARES

Yield: 2 to 3 dozen

2 cups all-purpose flour
¼ tsp. salt
¾ cup vegetable shortening
1 cup granulated sugar

1 large egg
1 tsp. vanilla extract
1½ cups shredded coconut
1 jar (10 oz.) cherry preserves

1. Preheat the oven to 350 degrees. Lightly grease a 13 by 9-inch baking pan.
2. Combine the flour and salt.
3. In a large bowl, cream the vegetable shortening and sugar. Beat in the egg. Beat in the vanilla extract. Gradually blend in the dry ingredients. Fold in the coconut.
4. Press ¾ of the dough evenly into the prepared baking pan. Spread the cherry preserves over the dough. Crumble the remaining dough over the preserves.
5. Bake for 25 to 30 minutes, until firm and lightly colored on top. Cool in the pan on a wire rack before cutting into large or small bars.

CHEWY PECAN BARS

Yield: 1 to 2 dozen

1 cup all-purpose flour
½ tsp. baking powder
1 tbsp. ground cinnamon
¼ tsp. salt
1 cup vegetable shortening

1 cup granulated sugar
2 large egg yolks
topping
2 large egg whites
1½ tsp. powdered sugar
1 cup pecans, chopped

1. Preheat the oven to 300 degrees.
2. Combine the flour, baking powder, cinnamon, and salt.
3. In a large bowl, cream the vegetable shortening and sugar. Beat in the large egg yolks. Gradually blend in the dry ingredients. Spread the dough evenly into a 13 by 9-inch baking pan.
4. To make the topping, beat the large egg whites in a medium bowl, until stiff and frothy. Fold in the powdered sugar. Spread the topping over the dough. Sprinkle the chopped pecans over the top.
5. Bake for 40 to 45 minutes, or until the topping is lightly colored. Cool in the pan on a wire rack before cutting into large or small bars.

CHOCOLATE CHIP BAR COOKIES

Yield: 2 to 3 dozen

2 cups all-purpose flour
1 tsp. baking powder
¼ tsp. baking soda
¼ tsp. salt
1 cup vegetable shortening
1½ cups packed light brown sugar
2 large eggs
2 tbsp. milk
1 tsp. vanilla extract
1 cup (6 oz.) semi-sweet chocolate chips

1. Preheat the oven to 350 degrees. Lightly grease a 9-inch square baking pan.
2. Combine the flour, baking powder, baking soda, and salt.
3. In a large bowl, cream the vegetable shortening and brown sugar. Beat in the eggs. Beat in the milk and vanilla extract. Gradually blend in the dry ingredients. Fold in the chocolate chips.
4. Spread the dough evenly in the prepared baking pan.
5. Bake for 25 to 30 minutes, or until golden brown on top. Cool in the pan on a wire rack before cutting into large or small bars.

Baking note: For an unusual variation, substitute white crème de menthe for the vanilla extract.

CHOCOLATE CHIP SQUARES

Yield: 3 to 5 dozen

crust
2¼ cups all-purpose flour
1 tsp. baking soda
½ tsp. salt
1 cup canola oil
½ cup granulated sugar
¾ cup packed light brown sugar
1 large egg
2½ tsp. white crème de menthe
1⅓ cups (8 oz.) semi-sweet chocolate chips

topping
½ cup (3 oz.) semi-sweet chocolate chips

1. Preheat the oven to 350 degrees. Lightly grease a 13 by 9-inch baking pan.
2. Combine the flour, baking soda, and salt.
3. In a large bowl, beat the canola oil and the two sugars. Beat in the egg. Beat in the crème de menthe. Gradually blend in the dry ingredients. Fold in the chocolate chips.
4. Spread the dough evenly in the prepared pan. Bake for 15 to 20 minutes, until the top is golden brown.
5. For the topping, spread the chocolate chips over the hot cookies. With a spatula, spread the melted chocolate chips evenly over the top. Cool in the pan on a wire rack before cutting into large or small bars.

CHOCOLATE DELIGHT BARS

Yield: 1 to 2 dozen

crust
½ cup butter, at room temperature
3 tbsp. powdered sugar
2 large egg yolks
1 tsp. instant coffee crystals
1 tbsp. warm water
2 cups all-purpose flour

topping
½ cup semi-sweet chocolate chips
2 large egg whites
¼ cup granulated sugar
¼ cup almonds, ground fine
¼ cup almonds, chopped

1. Preheat the oven to 350 degrees. Lightly grease a 9-inch square baking pan.
2. In a large bowl, combine the butter, powdered sugar, egg yolks, coffee crystals, and water and beat until well blended. Gradually blend in the flour. The mixture will be crumbly.
3. Press the mixture evenly into the bottom of the prepared baking pan. Bake for 20 minutes.
4. Meanwhile, melt the chocolate in the top of a double boiler, stirring until smooth. Remove from the heat.
5. In a medium bowl, beat the egg whites until foamy. Gradually beat in the sugar and beat until the whites hold stiff peaks. In a steady stream, beat in the melted chocolate. Fold in the ground almonds.
6. Spread the topping over the warm crust. Sprinkle with the chopped almonds and bake for 20 minutes longer, until set.

CHUNKY CHOCOLATE BROWNIES

Yield: 1 to 2 dozen

- ½ cup plus 2 tbsp. vegetable shortening
- ¼ cup unsweetened cocoa powder
- 1 cup granulated sugar
- 2 large eggs
- 1 tsp. vanilla extract
- ⅔ cup all-purpose flour
- 2½ oz. milk chocolate, cut into small chunks
- 2½ oz. white chocolate, cut into small chunks
- ¾ cup chocolate glaze
- 12 to 24 walnut halves for decoration

1. Preheat the oven to 350 degrees. Lightly grease a 9-inch square baking pan.
2. In the top of a double boiler, melt the vegetable shortening with the cocoa powder, stirring until smooth. Remove from the heat and beat in the sugar. Beat in the eggs and vanilla extract. Gradually blend in the flour. Fold in the milk and white chocolate chunks. Spread the mixture evenly in the prepared baking pan.
3. Bake for 18 to 20 minutes until firm to the touch.
4. Spread the chocolate glaze over the top. Cut into large or small bars, then place a walnut in the center of each. Cool in the pan on a wire rack.

CITRUS BARS

Yield: 2 to 3 dozen

2½ cups all-purpose flour
2 tsp. baking powder
1 tsp. baking soda
½ tsp. ground cinnamon
¼ tsp. ground cloves
¼ cup vegetable shortening
2 large eggs
1½ cups grapefruit juice
1 tsp. orange extract
1 cup cranberries, chopped
1 cup walnuts, chopped
topping
¾ cup flaked coconut
¾ cup crushed pineapple, drained

1. Preheat the oven to 350 degrees. Lightly grease a 13 by 9-inch baking pan.
2. Combine the flour, baking powder, baking soda, and spices.
3. In a large bowl, beat the vegetable shortening, eggs, grapefruit juice, and orange extract. Gradually blend in the dry ingredients. Fold in the cranberries and walnuts.
4. Spread the mixture evenly in the prepared baking pan. Sprinkle the coconut and pineapple over the top.
5. Bake for 20 to 25 minutes, until firm to the touch. Cool in the pan on a wire rack before cutting into large or small bars.

COCONUT BROWNIES

Yield: 1 to 2 dozen

¾ cup all-purpose flour
½ tsp. baking powder
¼ tsp. salt
½ cup vegetable shortening
1 cup granulated sugar

2 large eggs
1½ tbsp. chocolate syrup
1 tsp. vanilla extract
1 cup grated fresh
   (or packaged) coconut

1. Preheat the oven to 400 degrees. Lightly grease a 9-inch square baking pan.
2. Combine the flour, baking powder, and salt.
3. In a large bowl, cream the vegetable shortening and sugar. Beat in the eggs. Beat in the chocolate syrup and vanilla extract. Gradually blend in the dry ingredients. Fold in the coconut. Spread the mixture evenly in the prepared baking pan.
4. Bake for 30 to 35 minutes, until a toothpick inserted in the center comes out clean. Cool in the pan on a wire rack before cutting into large or small bars.

COCONUT CARAMEL BARS

Yield: 1 to 2 dozen

crust
- ½ cup vegetable shortening
- ½ cup powdered sugar
- 1 cup all-purpose flour

topping
- 1 can (14 oz.) sweetened condensed milk
- 1 cup (6 oz.) butterscotch chips
- 1 cup flaked coconut
- 1 tsp. vanilla extract

1. Preheat the oven to 350 degrees. Lightly grease a 9-inch square baking pan.
2. To make the crust, cream the vegetable shortening and powdered sugar in a medium bowl. Gradually work in the flour. Press the mixture evenly into the prepared baking pan.
3. Bake for 14 minutes.
4. Meanwhile, make the topping: In a large bowl, combine the condensed milk, butterscotch chips, coconut, and vanilla extract and stir until well blended.
5. Pour the topping mixture over the hot crust. Bake for 25 to 30 minutes longer, until a toothpick inserted in the center comes out clean. Cool in the pan on a wire rack before cutting into large or small bars.

COCONUT CHEWIES

Yield: 1 to 2 dozen

2 cups all-purpose flour
1 tsp. baking powder
½ tsp. salt
⅔ cup vegetable shortening
2 cups packed light brown sugar
3 large eggs
1 tsp. vanilla extract
1½ cups (9 oz.) semi-sweet chocolate chips
¾ cup walnuts, chopped
½ cup shredded coconut

1. Preheat the oven to 350 degrees. Lightly grease a 9-inch square baking pan.
2. Combine the flour, baking powder, and salt.
3. In a large bowl, cream the vegetable shortening and brown sugar. Beat in the eggs. Beat in the vanilla extract. Gradually blend in the dry ingredients. Fold in the chocolate chips, walnuts, and coconut. Spread the mixture evenly in the prepared baking pan.
4. Bake for 20 to 25 minutes, until firm to the touch. Cool in the pan on a wire rack before cutting into large or small bars.

DATE HONEY FINGERS

Yield: 4 to 5 dozen

¾ cup all-purpose flour
½ tsp. baking powder
Pinch of salt
¼ cup butter, at room temperature
5 tbsp. honey

2 large eggs
⅔ cup dates, pitted and chopped
½ cup walnuts, chopped fine
Powdered sugar for sprinkling

1. Preheat the oven to 375 degrees. Lightly grease an 8-inch square baking pan.
2. Combine the flour, baking powder, and salt.
3. In a large bowl, beat the butter and honey until smooth. Beat in the eggs. Gradually blend in the dry ingredients. Fold in the dates and walnuts. Spread the dough evenly in the prepared baking pan.
4. Bake for 25 to 30 minutes, until firm to the touch. Cool in the pan on a wire rack.
5. Sprinkle the cookies with powdered sugar and cut into finger-sized bars.

DUTCH CRUNCH APPLESAUCE BARS

Yield: 1 to 2 dozen

2 cups all-purpose flour
2 tsp. baking powder
1 tsp. anise seeds
¼ tsp. salt

½ cup butter, at room temperature
¾ cup granulated sugar
1 cup milk
½ cup almonds, chopped

1. Preheat the oven to 400 degrees. Lightly grease 2 baking sheets.
2. Combine the flour, baking powder, anise, and salt.
3. In a large bowl, cream the butter and sugar. Beat in the milk. Gradually blend in the dry ingredients. Fold in the almonds.
4. Drop the dough by spoonfuls 1½ inches apart onto the prepared baking sheets.
5. Bake for 10 to 12 minutes, or until lightly colored. Transfer to wire racks to cool.

ENGLISH TOFFEE BARS

Yield: 1 to 2 dozen

2 cups all-purpose flour
1 tsp. ground cinnamon
1 cup vegetable shortening
1 cup packed light brown sugar
1 large egg yolk
1 cup black or regular walnuts, chopped

1. Preheat the oven to 275 degrees. Lightly grease a 9-inch square baking pan.
2. Combine the flour and cinnamon.
3. In a large bowl, cream the vegetable shortening and brown sugar. Beat in the egg yolk. Gradually blend in the dry ingredients. Fold in the walnuts. Spread the mixture evenly in the prepared baking pan.
4. Bake for 55 to 60 minutes, until firm to the touch. Cool in the pan on a wire rack before cutting into large or small bars.

FRUIT-FILLED OATCAKES

Yield: 1 to 3 dozen

1½ cups rolled oats
½ tsp. baking soda
½ tsp. salt
½ cup vegetable shortening

1 cup packed light brown sugar
Fruit filling (your choice of jam or preserves)

1. Preheat the oven to 350 degrees. Lightly grease a 13 by 9-inch baking pan.
2. Cream the flour, rolled oats, baking soda, and salt.
3. In a large bowl, cream the vegetable shortening and brown sugar. Gradually blend in the dry ingredients.
4. Spread half the dough evenly into the prepared pan. Spread the fruit filling over the dough and press the remaining dough over the top of the fruit.
5. Bake for 20 to 25 minutes, until lightly colored on top. Cool in the pan on a wire rack before cutting into large or small bars.

Baking note: You can dress up these bars with a drizzle of white or lemon frosting.

FRUIT MERINGUE BARS

Yield: 1 to 4 dozen

crust
¾ cup vegetable shortening
¼ cup granulated sugar
2 large egg yolks
1½ cups all-purpose flour
topping
2 large egg whites, beaten
½ cup granulated sugar
1 cup almonds, chopped
filling
1 cup raspberry purée
   (see Baking note)
1 cup flaked coconut

1. Preheat the oven to 350 degrees. Lightly grease a 13 by 9-inch baking pan.
2. To make the crust, cream the vegetable shortening and sugar in a medium bowl. Beat in the egg yolks. Gradually blend in the flour. Press the dough evenly into the prepared baking pan.
3. Bake for 15 minutes.
4. Meanwhile, make the topping: In a medium bowl, beat the egg whites until foamy. Fold in the sugar and almonds.
5. Spread the raspberry purée over the hot crust. Sprinkle the coconut over the purée. Spread the topping over the coconut.
6. Bake for 20 to 25 minutes longer until the topping is set and lightly colored. Cool in a pan on a wire rack before cutting into large or small bars.

Baking note: To make raspberry purée, place defrosted and drained frozen raspberries in a blender and purée.

FUDGE BROWNIES I

Yield: 1 to 2 dozen

½ cup vegetable shortening
2 oz. semi-sweet chocolate, chopped
2 cups granulated sugar
4 large egg yolks
1¼ tsp. vanilla extract
1 cup all-purpose flour
1 cup walnuts, chopped

1. Preheat the oven to 325 degrees. Lightly grease a 9-inch square baking pan.
2. In the top of a double boiler, melt the vegetable shortening and chocolate, stirring until smooth. Remove from the heat and beat in the sugar. Beat in the egg yolks one at a time. Beat in the vanilla extract. Gradually blend in the flour. Fold in the nuts. Spread the batter evenly in the prepared baking pan.
3. Bake for 25 to 30 minutes, until a toothpick inserted in the center comes out clean. Cool in the pan on a wire rack before cutting into large or small bars.

Baking note: If you wish, frost with the icing of your choice before cutting into bars.

FUDGE BROWNIES II

Yield: 1 to 2 dozen

1⅓ cups all-purpose flour
¾ cup unsweetened
  cocoa powder
¼ tsp. salt
⅔ cup vegetable oil

2 cups granulated sugar
2 large eggs
1 tsp. almond extract
½ cup almonds, chopped

1. Preheat the oven to 350 degrees. Lightly grease a 13 by 9-inch square baking pan.
2. Combine the flour, cocoa powder, and salt.
3. In a large bowl, beat the vegetable oil and sugar together. Beat in the eggs one at a time. Beat in the almond extract. Gradually blend in the dry ingredients. Stir in the almonds. Spread the mixture evenly into the prepared baking pan.
4. Bake for 25 to 30 minutes, until a toothpick inserted in the center comes out clean. Cool in the pan on a wire rack before cutting into large or small bars.

Baking note: If you wish, frost with the icing of your choice before cutting into bars.

FUDGE BROWNIES III

Yield: 1 to 2 dozen

¾ cup all-purpose flour
½ tsp. baking powder
½ tsp. salt
6 oz. bittersweet chocolate, chopped

⅓ cup vegetable shortening
1 cup granulated sugar
2 large eggs
⅓ cup walnuts, chopped

1. Preheat the oven to 350 degrees. Lightly grease a 9-inch square baking pan.
2. Combine the flour, baking powder, and salt.
3. In the top of a double boiler, melt the chocolate and vegetable shortening, stirring until smooth. Remove from the heat and beat in the sugar. Beat in the eggs one at a time. Gradually blend in the dry ingredients. Fold in the walnuts.
4. Spread the batter evenly in the prepared pan.
5. Bake for 30 to 35 minutes, until a toothpick inserted in the center comes out clean. Cool in the pan on a wire rack before cutting into large or small bars.

Baking note: If you wish, frost with the icing of your choice before cutting into bars.

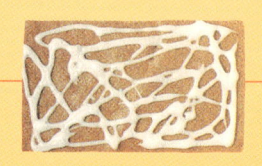

GINGER BARS

Yield: 1 to 4 dozen

1½ cups all-purpose flour
½ tsp. ground cinnamon
½ tsp. ground nutmeg
½ tsp. salt
½ tsp. baking soda
½ cup hot water

½ cup butter, at room temperature
½ cup packed light brown sugar
2 large eggs
½ cup molasses
Vanilla icing

1. Preheat the oven to 350 degrees. Lightly grease a 13 by 9-inch baking pan.
2. Combine the flour, spices, and salt.
3. In a small bowl, dissolve the baking soda in the hot water. Stir in the molasses.
4. In a large bowl, cream the butter and brown sugar. Beat in the eggs. Beat in the molasses mixture. Gradually blend in the dry ingredients. Spread the dough evenly in the prepared baking pan.
5. Bake for 18 to 20 minutes, or until a toothpick inserted in the center comes out clean.
6. Frost the warm cookies with icing. Let cool before cutting into large or small bars.

GRAHAM CRACKER BROWNIES I

Yield: 1 to 2 dozen

1½ cups graham cracker crumbs
¾ cup semi-sweet chocolate chips
½ cup almonds, chopped
½ cup shredded coconut
1 can (14 oz.) sweetened condensed milk

1. Preheat the oven to 350 degrees. Lightly grease a 9-inch square baking pan.
2. In a large bowl, combine all of the ingredients and blend well. Spread the mixture evenly in the prepared baking pan.
3. Bake for 20 to 25 minutes, until firm to the touch. Cool in the pan on a wire rack before cutting into large or small bars.

GRAHAM CRACKER BROWNIES II

Yield: 1 to 2 dozen

¾ cup vegetable shortening
¼ cup peanut butter
1 cup granulated sugar
2 large eggs
2½ cups graham cracker crumbs
2 cups miniature marshmallows
1 tsp. vanilla extract

topping
1 cup (6 oz.) semi-sweet chocolate chips
⅓ cup peanuts, ground fine

1. Lightly grease a 9-inch square baking pan.
2. In the top of a double boiler, melt the vegetable shortening with the peanut butter. Beat in the sugar. Remove from the heat and beat in the eggs one at a time. Return to the heat and cook, stirring, until the mixture thickens. Remove from the heat and stir in the graham crackers, marshmallows, and vanilla extract.
3. Spread the mixture evenly into the prepared baking pan. Chill for 2 hours.
4. To make the topping, melt the chocolate chips in a double boiler over low heat, stirring until smooth. Remove from the heat and stir in the ground peanuts.
5. Spread the topping evenly over the chilled brownies. Chill for 1 hour before cutting into large or small bars.

GRANOLA BARS

Yield: 3 to 4 dozen

6 cups rolled oats
1 cup shredded coconut
1 cup wheat germ
1 cup golden raisins
½ cup sunflower seeds
¼ cup sesame seeds, toasted

1 tsp. ground allspice
1 cup honey
¾ cup canola oil
⅓ cup water
1½ tsp. vanilla extract

1. Preheat the oven to 350 degrees. Lightly grease a 13 by 9-inch baking pan.
2. Combine the oats, coconut, wheat germ, raisins, sunflower seeds, sesame seeds, and allspice in a large bowl.
3. In a saucepan, combine the honey, oil, and water and heat. Remove from the heat and stir in the vanilla extract. Add to the dry ingredients and stir to coat well. Spread the mixture evenly in the prepared baking pan.
4. Bake for 30 to 40 minutes, until firm to the touch and no longer sticky. Transfer to wire racks to cool before cutting into large or small bars.
5. To store, wrap the bars individually in waxed paper.

GUMDROP BARS

Yield: 2 to 3 dozen

2 cups all-purpose flour
1 tsp. ground cinnamon
¼ tsp. salt
3 large eggs
2 cups packed light brown sugar
¼ cup evaporated milk
1 cup walnuts, chopped
1 cup gumdrops, chopped
Vanilla icing (optional—see Baking note)

1. Preheat the oven to 325 degrees. Lightly grease a 9-inch square baking pan.
2. Combine the flour, cinnamon, and salt.
3. In a large bowl, beat the eggs until thick and light-colored. Beat in the brown sugar. Beat in the milk. Gradually blend in the dry ingredients. Stir in the walnuts and gumdrops. Spread the dough evenly in the prepared baking pan.
4. Bake for 30 to 35 minutes, until lightly colored on top. Transfer to wire racks to cool.

Baking note: For a whimsical look, frost the bars with vanilla icing and decorate with gumdrops.

HAZELNUT SQUARES

Yield: 1 to 2 dozen

crust
1 cup all-purpose flour
¼ tsp. salt
¼ cup vegetable shortening

topping
2 tbsp. all-purpose flour
¼ tsp. salt
2 large eggs
¾ cup granulated sugar
1 tsp. rum
2 cups flaked coconut
1 cup hazelnuts, chopped

1. Preheat the oven to 350 degrees. Lightly grease a 9-inch square baking pan.
2. To make the crust, combine the flour and salt in a medium bowl. Cut in the vegetable shortening until the mixture resembles coarse crumbs. Press evenly into the prepared baking pan.
3. Bake for 15 minutes.
4. Meanwhile, make the topping: Combine the flour and salt.
5. In a medium bowl, beat the eggs and sugar until thick. Beat in the rum. Gradually blend in the dry ingredients. Stir in the coconut and hazelnuts.
6. Spread the topping over the top of the hot crust. Bake for 15 minutes longer, or until firm to the touch. Cool in the pan on a wire rack before cutting into large or small bars.

HELLO DOLLY COOKIES

Yield: 1 to 2 dozen

1 cup graham cracker crumbs
1 cup (6 oz.) semi-sweet chocolate chips
1 cup walnuts, chopped
1 cup shredded coconut
¼ cup butter, melted
1 can (14 oz.) sweetened condensed milk

1. Preheat the oven to 350 degrees. Lightly grease a 9-inch square baking pan.
2. Combine the graham crackers, chocolate chips, walnuts, and coconut in a medium bowl.
3. Pour the melted butter over the dry ingredients and stir. Press the mixture evenly into the prepared baking pan. Drizzle the condensed milk over the top.
4. Bake for 25 to 30 minutes, until lightly colored on top. Cool in the pan on a wire rack before cutting into large or small bars.

Baking note: Other cookies, such as chocolate or vanilla wafers, can be substituted for graham cracker.

HIKER'S TREATS

Yield: 1 to 2 dozen

¾ cup all-purpose flour
½ cup rolled oats
¼ cup toasted wheat germ
6 tbsp. packed light brown sugar
1 tbsp. grated orange zest
½ cup vegetable shortening

topping
2 large eggs
6 tbsp. packed light brown sugar
½ cup shredded coconut
⅔ cup slivered almonds

1. Preheat the oven to 350 degrees. Lightly grease an 8-inch square baking pan.
2. Combine the flour, oats, wheat germ, brown sugar, and orange zest in a bowl. Cut in the vegetable shortening until the mixture resembles coarse crumbs. Press the dough evenly into the prepared baking pan.
3. To make the topping, in a medium bowl, beat the eggs with the brown sugar until thick. Stir in the coconut. Pour over the dough and sprinkle the almonds over the top.
4. Bake for 30 to 35 minutes, until lightly colored on top and firm to the touch. Cool in the pan on wire rack before cutting into large or small bars.

Baking note: To enhance the flavor of these bars, add ¼ teaspoon almond extract to the topping. Raisins may be added to the dough.

HONEY BROWNIES

Yield: 2 dozen

¾ cup all-purpose flour
2 tbsp. unsweetened cocoa powder
¾ tsp. baking powder
¼ tsp. salt

⅓ cup plus 2 tbsp. vegetable shortening
¾ cup honey
2 large eggs

1. Preheat the oven to 325 degrees. Lightly grease an 8-inch square baking pan.
2. Combine the flour, cocoa powder, baking powder, and salt.
3. In a saucepan, melt the vegetable shortening with the honey. Remove from the heat and beat in the eggs one at a time. Gradually blend in the dry ingredients. Spread the batter evenly into the prepared baking pan.
4. Bake for 25 to 30 minutes, or until a toothpick inserted in the center comes out clean. Cool in the pan on a wire rack before cutting into large or small bars.

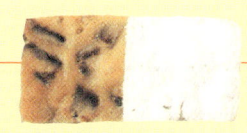

HONEY DATE BARS

Yield: 1 to 3 dozen

¾ cup all-purpose flour
¾ tsp. baking powder
¼ tsp. salt
3 tbsp. vegetable shortening
¾ cup honey

2 large eggs
1 cup dates, pitted and chopped
⅔ cup walnuts, chopped fine
Powdered sugar for coating

1. Preheat the oven to 350 degrees. Lightly grease a 9-inch square baking pan.
2. Combine the flour, baking powder, and salt.
3. In a large saucepan, melt the vegetable shortening with the honey, stirring until smooth. Remove from the heat and beat in the eggs one at a time. Gradually blend in the dry ingredients. Stir in the dates and walnuts. Spread the mixture evenly in the prepared baking pan.
4. Bake for 25 to 30 minutes, until lightly colored on top. Cool in the pan on a wire rack.
5. Cut into large or small bars, and dip half of each bar in powdered sugar.

JAM SQUARES

Yield: 1 to 3 dozen

crust
1½ cups all-purpose flour
¼ tsp. salt
½ cup butter
2 to 2½ tbsp. ice water

topping
2 large eggs
½ cup powdered sugar
2½ cups flaked coconut
⅓ cup raspberry preserves

1. Preheat the oven to 400 degrees.
2. To make the crust, combine the flour and salt in a medium bowl. Cut in the butter until the mixture resembles coarse crumbs. Add just enough water to make a soft dough. Press the dough evenly into an ungreased 9-inch square baking pan.
3. Bake for 20 minutes.
4. Meanwhile, make the topping: In a medium bowl, beat the eggs until thick and light-colored. Beat in the powdered sugar. Stir in the coconut.
5. Spread the raspberry preserves over the hot crust. Spread the topping over the preserves.
6. Bake for 20 to 25 minutes longer, until lightly colored on top and firm to the touch. Cool in the pan on a wire rack before cutting into large or small bars.

KENTUCKY PECAN BARS

Yield: 1 to 2 dozen

crust
1⅓ cups all-purpose flour
1¼ cups packed light brown sugar
½ tsp. baking soda
½ tsp. salt
1 cup pecans, toasted and chopped
½ cup vegetable shortening

topping
3 large eggs
⅓ cup granulated sugar
¼ cup butter, at room temperature
3 tbsp. bourbon
1 tsp. vanilla extract

1. Preheat the oven to 350 degrees. Lightly grease an 8-inch square baking pan.
2. To make the crust, combine the flour, brown sugar, baking soda, salt, and pecans. Cut in the vegetable shortening until the mixture resembles coarse crumbs. Press the mixture evenly into the prepared baking pans.
3. Bake for 15 minutes.
4. Meanwhile, make the topping: In a medium bowl, beat the eggs until thick and light-colored. Beat in the sugar and butter. Beat in the bourbon and vanilla extract.
5. Spread the topping over the hot crust. Bake for 20 to 25 minutes longer, until lightly colored and firm to the touch. Cool in the pan on a wire rack before cutting into large or small bars.

Baking note: You can decorate these bars by arranging pecan halves on the topping before baking.

KRISPIES
Yield: 1 to 2 dozen

1½ oz. milk chocolate
½ cup butter
½ cup corn syrup

1 cup powdered sugar
2 tsp. vanilla extract
4 cups crisp rice cereal

1. Lightly grease a 13 by 9-inch baking pan.
2. In a large saucepan, melt the chocolate and butter with the corn syrup, stirring until smooth. Remove from the heat and beat in the powdered sugar. Beat in the vanilla extract. Stir in the cereal. Press the mixture evenly into the prepared baking pan.
3. Chill in the refrigerator for 20 minutes or until set. Cut into large or small bars.

LEMON BARS I

Yield: 2 to 3 dozen

2½ cups all-purpose flour
2 tsp. baking powder
1 tsp. baking soda
½ tsp. ground allspice
¼ cup vegetable shortening
2 large eggs
1½ cups frozen lemon juice concentrate, thawed
1 tsp. lemon extract
1 cup golden raisins
1 cup walnuts, chopped
¾ cup flaked coconut
¾ cup canned crushed pineapple, drained

1. Preheat the oven to 350 degrees. Lightly grease a 13 by 9-inch baking pan.
2. Combine the flour, baking powder, baking soda, and allspice.
3. In a large bowl, cream the vegetable shortening until light and fluffy. Beat in the eggs. Beat in the lemon juice concentrate and lemon extract. Gradually blend in the dry ingredients. Fold in the raisins and walnuts. Spread the mixture evenly in the prepared baking pan. Sprinkle the coconut and pineapple over the top.
4. Bake for 20 to 25 minutes, until lightly colored on top and firm to the touch. Cool in the pan on a wire rack before cutting into large or small bars.

LEMON BARS II

Yield: 1 to 3 dozen

2 cups all-purpose flour
1 tsp. baking soda
1 tsp. ground cinnamon
½ tsp. ground nutmeg
½ tsp. salt
¾ cup vegetable shortening

1½ cups packed light brown sugar
2 large eggs
3 tbsp. fresh lemon juice
3 tbsp. grated lemon zest
1 cup raisins

1. Preheat the oven to 350 degrees. Lightly grease a 9-inch square baking pan.
2. Combine the flour, baking soda, spices, and salt.
3. In a large bowl, cream the vegetable shortening and brown sugar. Beat in the eggs one at a time. Beat in the lemon juice and zest. Stir in the raisins. Spread the dough evenly in the prepared baking pan.
4. Bake for 25 to 30 minutes, until lightly colored on top. Cool in the pan on a wire rack before cutting into large or small bars.

LEMON BARS III

Yield: 1 to 3 dozen

crust
2 cups all-purpose flour
½ cup powdered sugar
1 cup vegetable shortening
topping
4 large eggs
2 cups granulated sugar
⅓ cup fresh lemon juice
¼ cup all-purpose flour
½ tsp. baking powder

1. Preheat the oven to 350 degrees. Lightly grease a 13 by 9-inch baking pan.
2. To make the crust, combine the flour and powdered sugar in a medium bowl. Cut in the vegetable shortening until the mixture resembles coarse crumbs. Press the mixture evenly into the prepared baking pan.
3. Bake for 20 minutes.
4. Meanwhile, make the topping: In a large bowl, beat the eggs until thick and light-colored. Beat in the sugar. Beat in the lemon juice. Beat in the flour and baking powder.
5. Pour the topping over the hot crust. Bake for 20 to 25 minutes longer, until lightly colored on top and firm to the touch. Cool in the pan on a wire rack before cutting into large or small bars.

MACADAMIA NUT BARS

Yield: 1 to 3 dozen

crust
2 cups all-purpose flour
2 cups packed light brown sugar
1 cup vegetable shortening

filling
1 large egg
1 tsp. baking soda
1 cup sour cream
1 cup macadamia nuts, chopped

1. Preheat the oven to 350 degrees. Lightly grease a 13 by 9-inch baking pan.
2. To make the crust, combine the flour and brown sugar in a large bowl. Cut in the vegetable shortening until the mixture resembles coarse crumbs. Press evenly into the prepared baking pan.
3. To prepare the filling, in a medium bowl, beat the egg until thick and light-colored. Beat in the baking soda. Beat in the sour cream. Pour the filling over the crust. Sprinkle the chopped macadamia nuts over the top.
4. Bake for 45 to 50 minutes, or until firm to the touch. Cool in the pan on a wire rack before cutting into large or small bars.

MAGIC BARS

Yield: 1 to 3 dozen

1½ cups graham cracker crumbs
½ cup butter, melted

1 cup flaked coconut
1 cup (6 oz.) butterscotch chips
1 cup pecans, chopped

1. Preheat the oven to 350 degrees. Lightly grease a 13 by 9-inch baking pan.
2. Put the graham cracker crumbs in a large bowl and stir in the butter. Press the mixture into the prepared baking pan.
3. Combine the coconut, butterscotch chips, and pecans in a medium bowl and toss to mix. Spread this mixture evenly over the graham cracker mixture.
4. Bake for 25 to 30 minutes, until lightly colored on top. Cool in the pan on a wire rack before cutting into large or small bars.

MARBLED CREAM CHEESE BROWNIES

Yield: 1 to 3 dozen

4 oz. cream cheese, at room temperature
5 tbsp. vegetable shortening
1 cup granulated sugar
1 tbsp. cornstarch
3 large eggs
1½ tsp. vanilla extract
½ tsp. fresh lemon juice
½ cup all-purpose flour
½ tsp. baking powder
½ tsp. salt
⅔ cup semi-sweet chocolate chips

1. Preheat the oven to 350 degrees. Lightly grease a 9-inch square baking pan.
2. In a medium bowl, combine the cream cheese, 2 tablespoons of the vegetable shortening, ¼ cup of the sugar, and the cornstarch and beat until smooth. Beat in 1 of the eggs. Beat in ½ teaspoon of the vanilla extract and the lemon juice. Set aside.
3. Combine the flour, baking powder, and salt.
4. In the top of a double boiler, melt the chocolate and the remaining 3 tablespoons vegetable shortening, stirring until smooth. Remove from the heat and stir in the remaining 1 teaspoon of vanilla extract.
5. In a large bowl, beat the remaining 2 eggs and ¾ cup sugar. Beat in the cooled chocolate. Beat in the dry ingredients.
6. Spread the batter evenly in the prepared baking pan. Pour the cream cheese mixture over the top and swirl a knife back and forth a few times through the mixture to marble it.
7. Bake for 25 to 30 minutes, until a toothpick inserted in the center comes out clean. Cool in the pan on a wire rack before cutting into large or small bars.

MERINGUE-TOPPED BROWNIES

Yield: 1 to 3 dozen

2 cups all-purpose flour
1 tsp. baking powder
¼ tsp. baking soda
¼ tsp. salt
¼ cup vegetable shortening
¼ cup butter, at room temperature
½ cup granulated sugar
½ cup packed light brown sugar
2 large egg yolks
1 tbsp. strong brewed coffee
1½ tsp. crème de cacao
1½ cups (9 oz.) semi-sweet chocolate chips

topping
2 large egg whites
1 cup granulated sugar

1. Preheat the oven to 375 degrees. Lightly grease a 13 by 9-inch baking pan.
2. Combine the flour, baking powder, baking soda, and salt.
3. In a large bowl, cream the vegetable shortening, butter, and two sugars. Beat in the egg yolks. Beat in the coffee and crème de cacao. Gradually blend in the dry ingredients.
4. Spread the batter evenly in the prepared baking pan. Sprinkle the chocolate chips over the top.
5. To make the topping, in a bowl, beat the egg whites until foamy. Gradually beat in the sugar and beat until the whites form stiff peaks. Spread the topping over the chocolate chips.
6. Bake for 20 to 25 minutes, until lightly colored and firm to the touch. Cool in the pan on a wire rack before cutting into large or small bars.

MINT BROWNIES

Yield: 1 to 2 dozen

½ cup vegetable shortening
3 oz. bittersweet chocolate, chopped
2 cups granulated sugar
4 large egg yolks
½ tsp. vanilla extract
⅛ tsp. mint extract
1 cup all-purpose flour
1 cup walnuts, chopped

1. Preheat the oven to 325 degrees. Lightly grease a 9-inch square baking pan.
2. In the top of a double boiler, melt the vegetable shortening and chocolate, stirring until smooth. Remove from the heat and stir in the sugar. Beat in the egg yolks. Beat in the vanilla and mint extracts. Gradually blend in the flour. Stir in the walnuts. Spread the mixture evenly in the prepared baking pan.
3. Bake for 25 to 35 minutes, or until a toothpick inserted in the center comes out clean. Cool in the pan on a wire rack before cutting into large or small bars.

MOCHA COFFEE BROWNIES

Yield: 1 to 2 dozen

2 oz. semi-sweet chocolate, chopped
⅓ cup vegetable shortening
¾ cup all-purpose flour
½ tsp. baking powder
¼ tsp. salt

2 large eggs
1 cup granulated sugar
1 tsp. vanilla extract
2½ tsp. instant mocha coffee crystals
½ cup walnuts, chopped

1. Preheat the oven to 375 degrees. Lightly grease an 8-inch square baking pan.
2. In a double boiler, melt the chocolate and vegetable shortening, stirring until smooth. Remove from the heat.
3. Combine the flour, brown sugar, and salt.
4. In a large bowl, beat the egg until thick and light-colored. Beat in the sugar. Beat in the melted chocolate mixture and vanilla extract. Gradually blend in the dry ingredients. Stir in the coffee crystals. Spread the mixture evenly in the prepared baking pan. Sprinkle the walnuts on top.
5. Bake for 20 to 25 minutes, until a toothpick inserted in the center comes out clean. Cool in the pan on a wire rack before cutting into large or small bars.

NO-BAKE OATMEAL BARS

Yield: 2 to 3 dozen

3 tbsp. vegetable shortening
3 cups miniature marshmallows
¼ cup honey
½ cup peanut butter
1 cup raisins
¼ cup rolled oats
½ cup peanuts, chopped

1. Lightly grease a 9-inch square baking pan.
2. In a large saucepan, combine the vegetable shortening, marshmallows, honey, and peanut butter and heat, stirring, until smooth. Remove from the heat and gradually blend in the raisins, oats, and peanuts.
3. Spread the mixture evenly in the prepared baking pan. Chill for at least 2 hours.
4. Cut into large or small bars and wrap individually in waxed paper.

Baking note: You can spread this mixture in a larger pan to make thinner bars. For a different version, plump the raisins in boiling water while heating the marshmallow mixture. Spread half of the mixture in the prepared pan. Drain the raisins, pat dry, and sprinkle over the marshmallow mixture. Then sprinkle the finely chopped peanuts, and spread the remaining marshmallow mixture on top.

ORANGE BARS

Yield: 2 to 3 dozen

2½ cups all-purpose flour
2 tsp. baking powder
1 tsp. baking soda
1 tsp. ground cardamom
2 large eggs
¼ cup vegetable shortening, melted

1½ cups frozen orange juice concentrate, thawed
1 tsp. orange liqueur
1 cup cranberries, chopped
1 cup almond, chopped
¾ cup shredded coconut

1. Preheat the oven to 350 degrees. Lightly grease a 13 by 9-inch baking pan.
2. Combine the flour, baking powder, baking soda, and cardamom.
3. In a large bowl, beat together the eggs, vegetable shortening, orange juice concentrate, and orange liqueur until smooth. Gradually blend in the dry ingredients. Stir in the cranberries and almonds. Spread the mixture evenly in the prepared baking pan and sprinkle the coconut over the top.
4. Bake for 20 to 25 minutes, until the top is lightly colored. Cool in the pan on a wire rack before cutting into large or small bars.

ORANGE-CRANBERRY BARS

Yield: 2 to 3 dozen

3 cups all-purpose flour
1 tbsp. baking powder
¼ tsp. salt
⅔ cup butter, at room temperature
1½ cups granulated sugar

2 large eggs
¼ cup frozen orange juice concentrate, thawed
1 tbsp. almond extract
1 tbsp. water
1 cup raisins, chopped

1. Preheat the oven to 375 degrees. Lightly grease 2 baking sheets.
2. Combine the flour, baking powder, and salt.
3. In a large bowl, cream the butter and sugar. Beat in the eggs. Beat in the orange juice concentrate and zest. Beat in the almond extract and water. Gradually blend in the dry ingredients. Fold in the raisins.
4. Drop the dough by spoonfuls 1½ inches apart onto the prepared baking sheets.
5. Bake for 10 to 12 minutes, until lightly colored. Transfer to wire racks to cool.

PEANUT BUTTER-BANANA SQUARES

Yield: 2 to 3 dozen

1 cup all-purpose flour
1 tsp. baking powder
1 tsp. baking soda
¼ cup peanut butter
1 cup mashed bananas
¼ cup banana-flavored yogurt
1 large egg
½ cup peanuts, chopped

1. Preheat the oven to 350 degrees. Lightly grease an 8-inch square baking pan.
2. Combine the flour, baking powder, and baking soda.
3. In a large bowl, beat the peanut butter, bananas, and yogurt until smooth. Beat in the egg. Gradually blend in the dry ingredients. Fold in the peanuts. Spread the mixture evenly in the prepared baking pan.
4. Bake for 18 to 20 minutes, until lightly colored on top and firm to the touch. Cool in the pan on a wire rack before cutting into large or small bars.

PEANUT BUTTER BARS I

Yield: 2 to 3 dozen

1½ cups all-purpose flour
½ tsp. salt
2 cups packed light brown sugar
1 cup peanut butter
⅔ cup vegetable shortening
3 large eggs
1 tsp. vanilla extract
Vanilla icing

1. Preheat the oven to 350 degrees. Lightly grease an 8-inch square baking pan.
2. Combine the flour and salt.
3. In a large bowl, beat the brown sugar, peanut butter, and vegetable shortening until smooth and creamy. Beat in the eggs. Beat in the vanilla extract. Gradually blend in the dry ingredients. Spread the mixture evenly into the prepared baking pan.
4. Bake for 30 to 35 minutes, until firm to the touch. Cool in the pan on a rack.
5. Drizzle the icing over the cookies and cut into large or small bars.

PEANUT BUTTER BARS II

Yield: 3 to 4 dozen

½ cup rolled oats
1 tsp. baking powder
½ tsp. salt
½ cup vegetable shortening
¾ cup packed light
   brown sugar

1 cup peanut butter
3 large eggs
½ cup milk
1 tsp. vanilla extract
1 cup (6 oz.) semi-sweet
   chocolate chips

1. Preheat the oven to 350 degrees.
2. Combine the flour, oats, baking powder, and salt.
3. In a large bowl, cream the vegetable shortening and brown sugar. Beat in the peanut butter. Beat in the eggs. Beat in the milk and vanilla extract. Gradually blend in the dry ingredients. Spread the mixture evenly into an ungreased 8-inch square baking pan.
4. Bake for 25 to 30 minutes, until lightly colored on top. Sprinkle the chocolate chips over the hot crust. Let sit for 1 to 2 minutes to melt the chocolate, then spread it evenly over the top with a spatula. Cool in the pan on a wire rack before cutting into large or small bars.

Baking note: Use peanut butter chips for topping to add even more peanut butter flavor. Raisins may be added to the dough if so desired.

PUMPKIN BARS

Yield: 1 to 2 dozen

2 cups all-purpose flour
2 tsp. baking powder
1 tsp. baking soda
2 tsp. ground cinnamon
½ tsp. ground ginger
½ tsp. ground cloves
½ tsp. ground nutmeg
¾ tsp. salt
4 large eggs
2 cups granulated sugar
¾ cup vegetable oil
1 can (16 oz.) solid pack pumpkin
Vanilla icing

1. Preheat the oven to 350 degrees. Lightly grease a 13 by 9-inch baking pan.
2. Combine the flour, baking powder, baking soda, spices, and salt.
3. In a large bowl, beat the eggs and sugar until thick and light-colored. Beat in the oil. Beat in the pumpkin. Gradually blend in the dry ingredients. Scrape the mixture into the prepared baking pan.
4. Bake for 30 to 35 minutes, until the edges pull away from the sides and the top springs back when lightly touched. Cool in the pan on a wire rack.
5. Frost the cooled cookies with the icing and cut into large or small bars.

RAISIN BARS

Yield: 3 to 4 dozen

3 cups all-purpose flour
½ tsp. baking soda
½ tsp. ground cinnamon
¼ tsp. ground cloves
½ tsp. salt
1 cup vegetable shortening
¾ cup granulated sugar
¾ cup packed light brown sugar
2 large eggs, lightly beaten
¼ cup fresh orange juice
1 cup raisins
1 cup flaked coconut

glaze
¾ cup powdered sugar
1 tbsp. plus 1 tsp. fresh orange juice
1 tsp. orange zest, chopped

1. Preheat the oven to 350 degrees. Lightly grease a 15 by 10-inch baking pan.
2. Combine the flour, baking soda, spices, and salt. Beat in the eggs. Beat in the orange juice. Gradually blend in the dry ingredients. Fold in the raisins and coconut. Spread the mixture evenly in the prepared pan.
4. Bake for 20 to 25 minutes, until lightly colored on top and firm to the touch.
5. Meanwhile, make the glaze: Combine the sugar, orange juice, and orange zest in a small bowl and stir until smooth.
6. Drizzle the glaze over the hot crust. Cool in the pan on a wire rack before cutting into large or small bars.

ROCKY ROAD BARS

Yield: 1 to 3 dozen

- ¼ cup all-purpose flour
- ½ cup walnuts, ground fine
- ¼ tsp. baking powder
- ⅛ tsp. salt
- 1 tbsp. vegetable shortening
- ⅓ cup packed light brown sugar
- ½ tsp. vanilla extract

topping
- 1 cup miniature marshmallows
- 1 cup (6 oz.) semi-sweet chocolate chips
- ½ cup walnuts, chopped

1. Preheat the oven to 350 degrees. Lightly grease an 8-inch square baking pan.
2. Combine the flour, walnuts, baking powder, and salt.
3. In a large bowl, cream the vegetable shortening and brown sugar. Beat in the vanilla extract. Gradually blend in the dry ingredients. Spread the mixture evenly in the prepared baking pan.
4. Bake for 15 minutes.
5. Meanwhile, make the topping: In a small bowl, combine the marshmallows, chocolate chips, and walnuts and toss to blend.
6. Spread the topping mixture evenly over the hot crust. Bake for 15 to 18 minutes longer, until the topping is melted and lightly colored. Cool in the pan on a wire rack before cutting into large or small bars.

SEVEN-LAYER COOKIES

Yield: 2 to 3 dozen

- 1 cup vegetable shortening
- 1 cup cookie crumbs, such as vanilla wafers or chocolate sandwich cookies
- 1 cup (6 oz.) semi-sweet chocolate chips
- 1 cup coconut
- 1 cup almonds, chopped
- 1 cup (6 oz.) butterscotch chips
- 1 can (14 oz.) sweetened condensed milk

1. Preheat the oven to 350 degrees.
2. Melt the vegetable shortening in a small saucepan and pour into a 13 by 9-inch baking pan. Sprinkle the cookie crumbs over the shortening. Sprinkle the chocolate chips over the crumbs, then sprinkle the coconut over the chocolate chips. Sprinkle almonds over the coconut and the butterscotch chips over the almonds. Drizzle the condensed milk over the top.
3. Bake for 20 to 30 minutes, until firm to the touch. Cool in the pan on a wire rack before cutting into large or small bars.

SOME-MORE BARS

Yield: 1 to 2 dozen

¾ cup vegetable shortening
⅓ cup granulated sugar
3 cups graham cracker crumbs
2 cups miniature marshmallows
1 cup (6 oz.) semi-sweet chocolate chips

1. Preheat the oven to 350 degrees. Lightly grease a 13 by 9-inch baking pan.
2. In a large bowl, cream the vegetable shortening and sugar. Gradually blend in the cookie crumbs. Press half of this mixture firmly into the prepared baking pan. Sprinkle the marshmallows and chocolate chips over the top. Crumble over the remaining crumb mix.
3. Bake for 8 to 10 minutes, until firm to the touch. Cool in the pan on a wire rack before cutting into large or small bars.

SPICE BARS

Yield: 2 to 3 dozen

1 cup all-purpose flour
¼ cup unsweetened cocoa powder
1 tsp. baking powder
1 tsp. ground cinnamon
½ tsp. ground cloves
½ tsp. ground allspice
Pinch of salt
¼ cup vegetable shortening
1 cup granulated sugar
3 large eggs
1 tsp. vanilla extract
½ cup raisins
½ cup walnuts, chopped

1. Preheat the oven to 350 degrees. Lightly grease a 13 by 9-inch baking pan.
2. Combine the flour, cocoa powder, baking powder, spices, and salt.
3. In a large bowl, cream the vegetable shortening and sugar. Beat in the eggs. Beat in the vanilla extract. Gradually blend in the dry ingredients. Fold in the raisins and walnuts. Spread the dough evenly in the prepared baking pan.
4. Bake for 20 to 30 minutes, until the tip of a knife inserted in the center comes out clean. Cool in the pan on a wire rack before cutting into large or small bars.

Baking note: If you want to frost these bars, do so while they are still warm.

STRAWBERRY MERINGUE BARS

Yield: 3 to 4 dozen

crust
¾ cup vegetable shortening
¼ cup granulated sugar
2 large egg yolks
1½ cups all-purpose flour

topping
2 large egg whites
½ cup granulated sugar
1 cup almonds, chopped

filling
1 cup strawberry purée
1 cup flaked coconut

1. Preheat the oven to 350 degrees. Lightly grease a 13 by 9-inch square baking pan.
2. To make the crust, cream the vegetable shortening and sugar in a large bowl. Beat in the egg yolks. Gradually blend in the flour. Spread the dough evenly in the bottom of the prepared baking pan.
3. Place the pan in the oven and bake for 15 minutes.
4. Meanwhile, make the topping: In a large bowl, beat the egg whites until foamy. Gradually beat in the sugar and beat in until the whites hold stiff peaks. Fold in the chopped nuts.
5. Spread the strawberry purée over the hot crust and sprinkle with the coconut. Spread the topping over the coconut.
6. Bake for 20 to 25 minutes longer, or until the topping is firm to the tough. Cool in the pan on a wire rack before cutting into large or small bars.

TEATIME FAVORITES

Yield: 2 to 3 dozen

½ cup all-purpose flour
1 cup almonds, ground
2 oz. semi-sweet chocolate, chopped
½ cup vegetable shortening
1 cup granulated sugar
2 large eggs
½ tsp. almond extract
Vanilla icing

1. Preheat the oven to 350 degrees. Lightly grease a 9-inch square baking pan.
2. Combine the flour and almonds.
3. In the top of a double boiler, melt the chocolate and vegetable shortening, stirring until smooth. Remove from the heat and beat in the sugar. Beat in the eggs one at a time, beating vigorously after each addition. Beat in the almond extract. Gradually blend in the dry ingredients. Spread the mixture evenly in the prepared baking pan.
4. Bake for 35 to 40 minutes, or until a toothpick inserted in the center comes out clean. Cool in the pan on a wire rack.
5. Frost the cooled cookies with the icing and cut into large or small bars.

Baking note: To make a different version of these cookies, bake in a 13 by 9-inch baking pan for 25 to 30 minutes. Let cool in the pan on a wire rack, then use cookie cutters to cut into fancy shapes and frost.

TORTA FREGOLOTTI

Yield: 1 to 3 dozen

2⅔ cups all-purpose flour
1 cup almonds, ground
Pinch of salt
1 cup vegetable shortening

1 cup granulated sugar
1 tsp. grated lemon zest
2 tbsp. fresh lemon juice
1 tbsp. brandy

1. Preheat the oven to 350 degrees. Lightly grease a 9-inch square baking pan.
2. Combine the flour, almonds, and salt.
3. In a large bowl, cream the vegetable shortening and sugar. Beat in the lemon zest. Gradually blend in the dry ingredients. Measure out ¼ cup of the mixture for the topping and set aside. Beat the lemon juice and brandy into the remaining dough. Press the dough into the prepared baking pan. Crumble the reserved mixture over the top.
4. Bake for 45 to 50 minutes, until golden brown on top. Cool in the pan on a wire rack before cutting into large or small bars.

TROPICAL BARS

Yield: 2 to 3 dozen

¾ cup all-purpose flour
¾ tsp. baking powder
½ tsp. salt
½ cup vegetable shortening
1 cup packed light brown sugar
2 large eggs
½ tsp. rum
8 oz. canned crushed pineapple, drained
¾ cup flaked coconut

1. Preheat the oven to 350 degrees. Lightly grease a 9-inch square baking pan.
2. Combine the flour, baking powder, and salt.
3. In a large bowl, cream the vegetable shortening and brown sugar. Beat in the eggs and rum. Gradually blend in the dry ingredients. Fold in the pineapple and coconut. Spread the mixture evenly in the prepared baking pan.
4. Bake for 25 to 30 minutes, until colored on top. Cool in the pan on a wire rack before cutting into large or small bars.

TROPICAL FRUIT BARS

Yield: 1 to 3 dozen

1¼ cups all-purpose flour
1 tsp. baking soda
1 tbsp. canola oil
2 large eggs
1 tbsp. pineapple juice, preferably fresh
1 tsp. frozen orange juice concentrate, thawed
1¾ cups crushed fresh (or canned) pineapple, drained
1 cup flaked coconut
¾ cup macadamia nuts, chopped

1. Preheat the oven to 350 degrees. Lightly grease a 13 by 9-inch baking pan.
2. Combine the flour and baking soda.
3. In a large bowl, beat the oil and eggs until thick and light-colored. Beat in the pineapple juice and orange juice concentrate. Gradually blend in the dry ingredients. Fold in the pineapple, coconut, and macadamia nuts. Spread the mixture evenly in the prepared baking pan.
4. Bake for 15 to 20 minutes, until lightly colored on top. Cool in the pan on a wire rack before cutting into large or small bars.

WALNUT BARS

Yield: 3 to 4 dozen

crust
1⅓ cups all-purpose flour
½ tsp. baking powder
½ cup packed light brown sugar
⅓ cup vegetable shortening
¼ cup walnuts, chopped
filling
3 tbsp. all-purpose flour
½ tsp. salt
¼ cup packed light brown sugar
2 large eggs
¾ cup dark corn syrup
1 tsp. vanilla extract
¾ cup walnuts, ground fine

1. Preheat the oven to 350 degrees. Grease a 13 by 9-inch baking pan.
2. To make the crust, combine the flour, baking powder, and brown sugar in a large bowl. Cut in the vegetable shortening until the mixture resembles coarse crumbs. Stir in the walnuts. Spread the mixture evenly in the prepared baking pan.
3. Bake for 10 minutes.
4. Meanwhile, make the filling: Combine the flour and salt. In a medium bowl, beat the brown sugar and eggs until thick and lightly colored. Beat in the corn syrup. Beat in the vanilla extract. Gradually blend in the dry ingredients. Pour the filling over the hot crust. Sprinkle the walnuts over the top. Bake for 25 to 30 minutes longer, until the top is firm to the touch. Cool in the pan on a wire rack before cutting into large or small bars.

WALNUT SQUARES

Yield: 2 to 3 dozen

crust
¾ cup vegetable shortening
⅓ granulated sugar
2 large egg yolks
1 tsp. vanilla extract
1½ cups all-purpose flour
filling
2 tbsp. all-purpose flour
¼ tsp. baking powder
¼ tsp. salt
1½ cups packed light brown sugar
2 large eggs, separated
2 tbsp. evaporated milk
1 tsp. vanilla extract
1 cup shredded coconut
½ cup walnuts, chopped

1. Preheat the oven to 350 degrees. Lightly grease a 9-inch square baking pan.
2. To make the crust, cream the vegetable shortening and sugar in a medium bowl. Beat in the egg yolks and vanilla extract. Gradually blend in the flour. Press the dough evenly into the prepared baking pan.
3. Bake for 12 minutes.
4. Meanwhile, make the topping: Combine the flour, baking powder, and salt.
5. In a large bowl, beat the brown sugar and eggs. Beat in the milk and vanilla extract. Gradually blend in the dry ingredients. Stir in the coconut and walnuts. Pour the topping over the hot crust. Bake for 20 minutes longer, or until the top is firm to the touch. Cool in the pan on a wire rack before cutting into large or small bars.

ZUCCHINI BARS

Yield: 2 to 3 dozen

2½ cups all-purpose flour
1 tsp. ground cinnamon
½ cup granulated sugar
½ cup vegetable oil
2 large eggs
¾ cup finely chopped zucchini
½ cup mashed, cooked carrots
1 cup pecans, chopped
⅓ cup raisins

1. Preheat the oven to 350 degrees. Lightly grease and flour a 13 by 9-inch baking pan.
2. Combine the flour and cinnamon.
3. In a large bowl, beat the sugar and vegetable oil together. Beat in the eggs one at a time. Beat in the zucchini and carrots. Gradually blend in the dry ingredients. Stir in the pecans and raisins. Spread the batter evenly in the prepared baking pan.
4. Bake for 20 to 25 minutes, until a toothpick inserted in the center comes out clean. Cool in the pan on a wire rack before cutting into large or small bars.

Choc. Amaretti Cake

3/4 C semi sweet chocolate

1 cup almonds

amaretti cookies 1 cup

pulse

1 stick unsalted butter
   (room temp)

2/3 c sugar

orange zest (2 tsp)

4 egg

add dry cookies &
   chocolate.

(springform pan)

350° 35 minutes

Creamsicle Mimosas

2 1/2 C orange juice
1 C. superfine sugar
1 C half & half
1 T orange zest

blend - freeze -
1 scoop to champagne

Margaritas
1 cup lime juice
1/2 C triple sec
1 scoop sugar (1/4 C)
1/2 C water
1/4 o. tequila
strawberries